AMPHORAS

AND THE ANCIENT WINE TRADE

AMERICAN SCHOOL OF CLASSICAL STUDIES

AT ATHENS · PRINCETON · NEW JERSEY

1979

EXCAVATIONS OF THE ATHENIAN AGORA
Picture Book No. 6
Revised Edition

Prepared by Virginia R. Grace
Photographs of the Agora Material
by Alison Frantz
Produced by The Meriden Gravure Company
Meriden, Connecticut
© American School of Classical Studies at Athens 1979

COVER: Silver coin of Chios, both sides (3:1). Compare with 46.
INSIDE COVER: Diver at an ancient wreck. Compare the amphora
with the latest in 62.
TITLE PAGE: Knidian Amphora Stamp, 188–167 B.C. (2:1).
BACK COVER: Silver coin of the Dionysians (?) in Macedonia about
500 B.C. (2:1).

EXCAVATIONS OF THE ATHENIAN AGORA
PICTURE BOOKS

These booklets are obtainable from the
American School of Classical Studies at Athens
c/o Institute for Advanced Study, Princeton, N.J. 08540, U.S.A.
They are also available in the Agora Museum, Stoa of Attalos, Athens
ISBN 87661–619–8

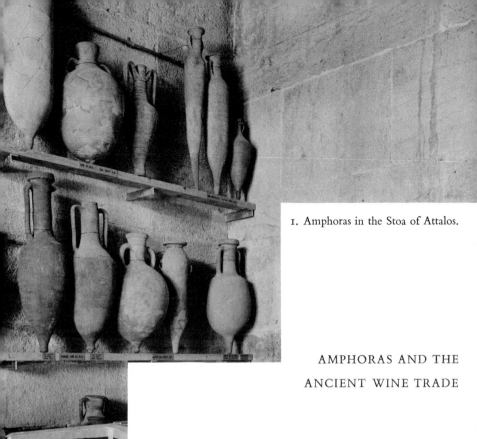

1. Amphoras in the Stoa of Attalos.

AMPHORAS AND THE
ANCIENT WINE TRADE

One of the shops of the reconstructed Stoa of Attalos in Athens houses a selection of the commercial containers found, whole or in fragments, in and about the ancient market place of Athens. These large, plain, two-handled clay jars (1) were called by ancient Greeks and Romans 'amphoras' though they had also other names in both Greece and Italy; this word, used also in French and Italian, is familiar nowadays from the reports of Captain Cousteau (*The Silent World*) and other divers describing the wrecked ancient cargoes found at the bottom of the sea off the coasts of southern France and northern Italy. Probably most of these large amphoras were made for the transport and storage of wine, though many were used for oil, preserved fish, pitch and other moist substances, including water.

There is a variety of shapes, but they have in common a mouth narrow enough to be corked, two opposite vertical handles and at bottom usually a tip or knob (2) which serves as a third handle, below

2. Knob handle on the bottom of a jar.

the weight, needed when one inverts a heavy vessel to pour from it. A flat bottom big enough for the jar to stand on would give no purchase for lifting. Attached bases like those on small two-handled vases for the table would add uselessly to the weight of these containers and to the inconvenience of stowing them as cargo, as well as to the cost of manufacture. Stands of various kinds were ordinary equipment for times and places when the jars needed to be upright, sometimes four-footed wooden ones (4, 8) or large pottery rings in which the body of the amphora sits as in an eggcup (5, 6).

Greek wine fermented in large nonportable jars called *pithoi*, from which it was drawn off into amphoras, while the Egyptians made theirs directly in the amphoras, hence the use of stands at the Egyptian vintage (4). For wine-making in Greece, see Picture Book Number 1, 14.

3. Pouring wate

4. Amphoras in footed wooden stands, at the vintage, Egypt. Late 4th century B.C. To the right, boys are trampling grapes in a winepress; the juice pours from a spout into a trough. The jars are of Phoenician (left, without necks) and Greek types.

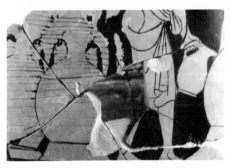

5, 6. Amphoras in clay ring supports, ancient drawing (5th century B.C.) and actual jar and stand (6th – early 5th centuries B.C.).

In ancient pictures wine jars appear regularly in stands at Egyptian and Syrian banquets, but rarely so at Greek parties, since the Greeks drank wine diluted with water, pouring it into mixing bowls for the feast (7), while the Syrians and Egyptians sucked from the jar, using bent tubes made of hollow reeds with metal angles (8).

Indeed, it was not often necessary for a Greek or Roman wine jar to be really vertical; when full, it would usually have been sealed, and when such jars are partly empty, a tilted position is more convenient for the next draught. As merchandise in warehouse or ship, or household supply in the cellar, the sealed jars leaned against walls or bulwarks and supported each other, perhaps partly sunk or otherwise fixed in place (14, 69).

7. Pouring wine.

8. A Syrian drinks through a bent tube. Note the small jar with ear-like handles; compare those in 14 and 15. Here the jar is set in a high stand. From the gravestone of a Syrian mercenary soldier who died in Egypt. 14th century B.C.

9. Little slave asleep against a tilted amphora. Terracotta figurine from a Greek city in southern Italy. Late 4th century B.C.

10. Amphoras at the spring, to fetch water for the ship Argo.

In the open, full jars might lean against a rock or be steadied by stones or sunk in the ground.

In an illustration of one of the adventures of the Argonauts, an engraving (10) on a bronze box made in Italy in the 4th century B.C., we see amphoras that have been brought to the spring, as water jars are still brought ashore to be filled by sailors of small Mediterranean craft. The central incident of the adventure appears on the other side of the box, before the ship Argo. On our side are shown the pleasures of dry land, the firm rocky ground, the flowering plants, above all, the abundant fresh water that gushes from a carved waterspout. The jars, like the two wide drinking cups, are indistinguishable from those used for wine, and we may suppose that they were old wine jars.

The Greek historian Herodotos (III, 5–7) reports the large-scale employment of secondhand wine jars for carrying water from Egypt to service the desert road to Syria. Herodotos learned this as a result of his astonishment at seeing no empty wine jars lying about in Egypt, although, as he observed, there was continual shipment of Greek and Phoenician wine into that country. He visited Egypt at about the middle of the 5th century B.C. A century and a half later, after

the breakup of the Persian empire and then of Alexander's, Egypt and Syria were no longer under a single administration, and road communications between them were not to the interest of any government. So we find the Greek and Phoenician empties servicing the vintage of a rich Egyptian named Petosiris, as sculptured on the walls of his tomb at Hermoupolis, halfway between Cairo and Luxor (4).

Obviously, under normal conditions amphoras did tend to accumulate, as gasoline cans do in some countries today, and to be adapted to many purposes. They were re-used for all sorts of commodities—cheese and pickled fish, beer, nuts, honey. Some became funerary urns; others, with a section cut from one side, served as coffins for infants. Whole or broken, their bulk was exploited in filling disused wells or cisterns, or in levelling a stretch of ground for a large building. Their hollowness and the degree of their fragility were used for strategic purposes, most memorably, as Herodotos tells us (VIII, 28), by the Phocians of central Greece, who dug a great pit in a mountain pass, laid in amphoras and covered them with earth, and so trapped the enemy cavalry, whose horses crashed in and broke their legs.

11. Container jars in a tomb in the land of Canaan where they were invented.

The idea of a two-handled pottery container made especially for transport seems to have originated with the Canaanites, forefathers of the Phoenicians, in the coastal area of later Syria and Palestine. Quantities of sturdy plain jars with small mouth, narrow base and opposite vertical handles have been found in tombs and settlements of the Bronze Age in Palestine and Syria. On the walls of Egyptian tombs (12) is shown how such jars were brought to the storehouses of Pharaoh, full of the goods of the conquered Canaanites; the clay sealings of the jars are in place, and sometimes hieroglyphs beside the pictures describe the contents, 'honey', 'honeyed wine', 'incense', 'olive oil', etc. In vessels of this kind Jacob sent to Joseph

12. Canaanite goods brought by the conquering Egyptians to their own storehouses. 15th and early 14th centuries B.C.

13. A Canaanite jar (right) in the tomb of an Athenian lady.

14. Warehouse in the port of ancient Ugarit, north Canaan.

'the best fruits of the land', honey, spices, myrrh (a kind of incense) and nuts. For honey and oil, we may read sugar and butter, staples of good living. Incense was also a prime commodity for the Egyptians, who had a special official in charge of the palace stock.

A few Canaanite jars reached Greece. Most of these look like the eighty-odd found in a warehouse of the port district of ancient Ugarit (14), with their angular shoulders and light-colored clay, as for instance a little jar (15) found lately among ruins of the last days of Mycenae. The site of Ugarit is near modern Latakia in Syria; evidently this variety is the produce of northern Canaan. Three jars made of coarse brown clay have a rounder shoulder and look like many found in tombs in southern Palestine, Jacob's country. One of these (13) comes from the tomb of a noble lady of the Late Bronze Age in Athens and is to be seen in the Agora Museum in the Stoa of Attalos, together with the other gifts found in her tomb.

15. Jar from north Canaan, found in Mycenae.

16. The Egyptians copied the Canaanite jar for their own bottling and preserving. Note the winepress above, left; compare 4. Late 15th century B.C.

The Egyptians adopted the form of the Canaanite jar, since it was much less awkward than their own invention, which had no handles. It was in Egypt, probably, that the two-handled container was first used on a large scale for wine (16). Although it served there for other stores as well, the bulk of the jars were no doubt made for the bottling of the various Egyptian vintages. Wines from particular vineyards were distinguished and named at a very early period; one that was considered choice nearly 5000 years ago seems to have come from the region of Lake Mareotis, west of Alexandria, which still today names a special brand.

Wine jars in Egypt were elaborately labelled by stamps and ink writing on the unbaked clay that was moulded over the mouth of the jar and left to harden as a stopper. Occasionally, however, the Egyptians employed a device used very early in Canaan and later standardized in the kingdom of Judah: an official stamp impressed on the handle of the jar before it was fired in the kiln (17, 18).

17. Stamp of Queen Nefertiti of Egypt, from the handle of a jar. 14th century B.C.

18. Royal stamp of the kingdom of Judah, on a jar handle. 7th century B.C. Below the beetle device read, right to left, HBRN, the ancient city of Hebron.

19.
Amphiphoreus.

Amphoras are referred to by their Greek name *amphiphoreus* or *amphoreus* on clay tablets of the Mycenean period, spelled out in the characters of the Linear B syllabary, often accompanied by an ideogram or small identifying sketch (19). Homer uses the word, for instance for the wine jars carried by Telemachos on his voyage from Ithaka to Pylos (*Odyssey* II, 290, 349, 379). By derivation, it means something which can be carried from both sides (20). Shipping amphoras that are 'pointed', that is, too narrow at the bottom to stand alone, were made in parts of the Greek world as early as the 7th century B.C. The idea of thus streamlining the jar for transport may have come to the Greeks from contact with the Phoenicians, who had continued to make an adaptation of the Canaanite jar; or it may have been suggested to them by what they saw in Egypt, where there were colonies of Greek merchants as early as the late 7th century B.C., and where Greek soldiers went far up the Nile in the service of an Egyptian king, Psammetichos II (594–588 B.C.), and cut their names on the colossal statues at Abu Simbel.

20.
Silver Coin. About 500 B.C.

Some 870 commercial amphoras have been put together from the excavations of the Athenian Agora, which was of course a market center. A selection exhibited in the Stoa of Attalos (1) covers more than a thousand years, from before 500 B.C. to the 6th century of our era. The jars are mostly imports; skins would normally be used for local transport. They came to Athens from many places, the names of some of which can be seen on the map in the middle of this booklet (34), while others remain to be identified. Like modern containers, these declare themselves by special shapes, and color also helps to distinguish them, though this varies somewhat with the firing of the individual pot. Some very common kinds are labelled also by stamp impressions made before firing, set usually on the tops of the handles, like the earlier stamps mentioned above (17, 18). The red clay and ringed tip of the Knidian jar in the foreground of Figure 1 are characteristic of its place of manufacture; but in addition the stamp (the same one on both handles) includes the word *knidion*, i.e. 'Knidian (jar)'.

21. Stamp marking a *knidion* of Xen-
okles. From jar in foreground of 1.
2nd century B.C.

23. Pair of rose stamps of the Rhodian manufacturer Hellanikos, dated in the term of Aristonidas, month Artamitios. Duplicates of the stamps on the jar to the left in 22.

22. Rhodian amphoras. 3rd century B.C.

24. Silver coin of Rhodes. 3rd century B.C.

25. Pair of rectangular stamps of the Rhodian manufacturer Agoranax, dated in the term of Sostratos, month Artamitios.

Creamy surface, peg tip and acute-angled handles identify amphoras from Rhodes, but they are marked also by pairs of stamps which often contain the 'rose' (23) or the rayed head of the sun-god Helios (25, left) which are used as emblems on the coins of Rhodes (24). On both Rhodian and Knidian jars the stamps contain two names, one an endorsement, perhaps by a licensed manufacturer, the other a date, 'in the term of so-and-so', usually an annually appointed official, the common way of expressing dates in those days. Amphoras from Sinope on the Black Sea and the earliest from the island of Thasos are similarly marked. On Rhodian jars the month also is given. Why amphoras were dated is not fully understood, but the chief purpose may have been to fix more closely the responsibility for their being containers of standard capacity, while one effect must have been to date the contents, identifying for instance the age or special vintage of the finer kinds of wine, and the freshness of the cheaper which were not worth drinking after a year. Traders and tax collectors had to recognize the make of a jar to know what capacity (within tolerances) was guaranteed, because standard containers were of different capacities in different states and at different dates; compare nowadays the British and United States gallons, and remember a change not long ago from the quart to the fifth for regulation containers of whiskey.

Actual sizes: the jar to the right in 22, two inches high in the picture, is about two and a half feet in actual height (0.78 m.) and holds a little under seven U.S. gallons (filled to the brim). Amphoras of the same (Rhodian) class are being handled in 3 and in 26. In the following pages, where commercial amphoras are shown without human scale, they are all at about one-fifteenth of their real size, like the jars in 22. Stamps and coins are shown at actual size, unless otherwise marked.

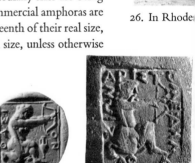

26. In Rhode[s]

States like Thasos, whose chief product was a famous wine, kept close control of production and sale. Standard measures have been found (29), and systematic stamping of the containers began very early (28). A good part of the Thasian wine laws can still be read in Thasos, inscribed in the marble slabs (30) that had been posted for the information of the ancient public.

27, 28. Silver coin and amphora stamp of Thasos. Early 4th century B.C. Herakles as Archer.

29. Standard wine measure in Thasos, with hollows for a quarter-amphora (left) and a half-amphora, labelled. 1st century B.C.

30. Part of a Thasian wine law. Early 5th century B.C.

The shaping and marking for easy recognition of these commercial containers makes them very good potential evidence for the history of trade; lines can be drawn from their known places of origin to the sites where they have been found. More or less *whole* imported stamped jars are relatively uncommon finds, but vast numbers of the stamped handles are found in ancient dumps and fillings. On the map (34) are shown some of the finding places. Sites of greatest mass discovery are Athens, where about 40,000 stamped handles have been collected of which 65 per cent or more are from Knidos, and Alexandria, where of almost 90,000 already counted at least 85 per cent are from Rhodes. One must divide by about one-half for the number of *jars*, since the majority had two stamps. The great development of the standard container in Rhodes, that is, the huge output and the fact that Rhodian jars were systematically marked during more than two centuries, must be partly accounted for by the port tax from which Rhodes drew a large proportion of her revenue. Wine carried in Rhodian and Knidian jars was not choice (like Thasian or Chian) but of ordinary grade consumed in bulk, for instance by the troops.

31. Amphoras from Rhodes (left) and from Roman Spain (?) found in debris of the destruction of Corinth in 146 B.C. The Roman jar is unstamped. The Rhodian is endorsed by Imas and dated in the term of Autokrates. In the background, columns of the temple of Apollo at Corinth, 6th century B.C.

32. In a shop in Pompeii, buried under ash in 79 A.D.

33. From deposits in the Athenian Agora dated 1st to early 2nd centuries A.D. Note the similarity of the jar to the right with one in 32. The shape is common in Athens at this period. Sometimes one handle bears a stamp with a Greek name.

Figures on finds in particular places naturally provide incomplete information. Before we can use such evidence, we need to know the periods during which import took place, the times when it was at its peak, etc. The ancients of course had reference lists of the dating authorities named on stamps, but the essential parts of these records have not been found. We must build up our own lists as well as possible from many clues. Chief among these are the finding places of certain of the jars and fragments. For instance, Carthage and Corinth were both completely destroyed in 146 B.C. and lay deserted for a century, so Greek stamped amphoras found in those places (31) were nearly all made earlier than the middle of the 2nd century B.C. Again, Pergamon under King Attalos I (241–197 B.C.) came to be on good terms with Rhodes though not during the first years of his reign; we know of the delay because Pergamon is not on the list of contributors to the rebuilding of Rhodes after the city was ruined in 226 B.C. (by the earthquake which knocked down the Colossus). Relations with Rhodes were broken off again at some time during the following reign at Pergamon, that of Eumenes II (197–159 B.C.). So it is fair to guess that 800 Rhodian stamped handles found together between the foundations of a building in Pergamon belong mostly to the late 3rd or early 2nd century B.C., and since they include about forty names of yearly officials, the over-all dates are given as 220–180 B.C. As evidence for dating jar shapes, though not stamps, may be mentioned the destruction of Pompeii and Herculaneum in 79 A.D.; several of the early Roman types found in the excavations of the Athenian Agora (33, 60) are matched by jars from under the ash and volcanic mud of those sites (32, 61).

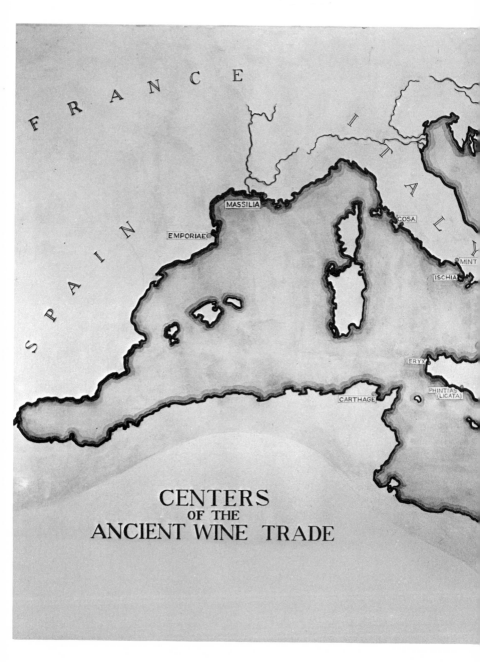

CENTERS
OF THE
ANCIENT WINE TRADE

34. The wine-producing states named on this map are mostly clustered around the Aegean and Black Seas: Rhodes, Knidos, Kos, Paros, Kolophon, Chios, Lesbos, Ikos, Mende, Thasos, Sinope, Chersonesos. The rest of the names mark some of the places where stamped handles of

imported containers have been found. For quantity of finds, no other places approach Athens (about 40,000) and Alexandria (nearly 90,000). Handles of foreign containers are also found on the sites of the producing states, but mostly in very restricted quantities.

35. From debris of the destruction of Athens by the Persians in 480–479 B.C. The small amphora to the left is Corinthian, perhaps also the bright one in front. None of these jars is stamped.

36. From debris of the destruction of Athens by the Romans in 86 B.C. For the Rhodian, Knidian and Chian to the left, see also 62, 64 and 47; the first two are stamped. The Roman jar at the right end has an incuse stamp on the shoulder reading SPE. The jars lean against the terrace parapet of the Stoa of Attalos. Behind them is the Market Hill of Athens and the temple of Hephaistos and Athena.

Like Corinth, Carthage and Pompeii, Athens also was destroyed, though less completely; the city was rebuilt after three destructions. Following the first two, the refuse, including broken amphoras, was swept into old wells and other pits, to be recovered by archaeologists in large groups of pottery which had all been in use at about the same time, a time made precise by the known date of the catastrophe. See opposite (35) six jars from such a group and a seventh from another, known by the figured vases found in the same wells with the jars to be refuse from the destruction of Athens by the Persians in 480 B.C.; figured vases of similar style were found under the mound at Marathon, raised ten years earlier over those who fell in that battle. The second general destruction of Athens, that by the Romans under Sulla in 86 B.C., left a vast amount of badly broken pottery, many samples of which have been restored to their original shapes, including the Rhodian, Knidian and Chian amphoras to the left in 36. The same event dates the solid Roman jar at the right end of the picture, which was possibly part of Sulla's commissary.

Following the third destruction, in 267 A.D. by the Herulians, a tribe from the north, the Athenians reduced the size of the city, building the fortification wall that incorporated, and thus saved, a large part of the Stoa of Attalos, and abandoning the destroyed houses on the west side of the Agora. From one of these ruined houses comes the tall jar in 37, which had brought wine or oil from northern Africa, also the big round jar to the right of it. The third item in 37 was found under the floor of one of the towers of the new fortification wall, hence must date not much later than 267 A.D.

37. The destruction of Athens in 267 A.D. dates these. None is stamped.

38. Agora group of the late 2nd century B.C.

In the long-continued habitation of Athens, between general disasters ordinary breakage produced in time the waste material with which disused wells and cisterns were filled or areas levelled. Accumulation of jars might start, while a well was in use, with those lost while being used to draw water. Or sometimes amphoras were laid as packing around the tile drums forming the shaft of a well driven down through the middle of an older cistern. Groups of pots or stamped handles found together in such fillings serve to date each other, like coins in a hoard. Of particular interest is a group used as packing for a well evidently constructed in the late 2nd century B.C., of which a selection is shown in 38. The tall Roman amphora at the left end is one of the first known to have carried wine from Italy to Greece.. Thousands like it have been found in ancient wrecks off the coasts of Italy and southern France. The Knidian beside it bears stamps that are among the earliest to name the pairs of commissioners (40) who add their endorsement to Knidian wine jars of the late 2nd and early 1st centuries B.C. (one of the latest pairs is named on the Knidian in 36; about twenty years apparently separate the two). The torpedo-shaped container at the right end of the picture belongs to a kind made in earlier times in Carthage; at least a stamp with Carthaginian characters appears on a fragmentary jar of the same class dated about 200 B.C. Since Carthage was in ruins in the late 2nd century, we may guess that this jar comes from one of her colonies, perhaps in

39, 40. Knidian stamps matching those on the second jar in 38.

41. Mystery stamp
on torpedo jar in 38.

Spain or the Balearic islands. The stamp on the shoulder (41), which has been identified as Semitic, has not been satisfactorily read. The round jar beside the torpedo raises a similar problem; its shape is reminiscent of earlier jars made in Corinth, though nothing closely like it has been found there. We may suppose that the pottery works, no doubt outside the city of Corinth proper, were spared in 146 B.C. or soon rebuilt, perhaps by citizens of neighboring Sikyon, and that they continued to produce for export.

A group of jars characteristic of Athens of the 3rd century B.C. is partly illustrated in 22, 23 and 25; of the four jars of the group, all stamped Rhodians, the shapes of two are shown and the stamps of the other two. In Athens, the 3rd century is the period of greatest import of Rhodian stamped jars; this import diminishes early in the 2nd century.

In 42 and 43 are selected jars from two groups respectively of the 4th and 5th centuries B.C. The latter is of special interest in that it gives us the date, in the third quarter of the 5th century, of a marked change in shape of the wine amphora of Chios.

42. Agora group of the 4th century B.C. The jar to the right has a monogram stamp.

43. Group of the third quarter of the 5th century B.C. Famous wine jars: Chian of old and new styles, and, in front, Mendean.

44.

Finds from such dated groups at the Agora make it possible to follow evolution in the shapes of many classes of amphoras. One of the most interesting is in fact the series from Chios, the changing form of the jar being faithfully depicted on the coins of this state. Note in the earlier jars (44) the development of the curious and very characteristic swelling in the neck. When in the third quarter of the 5th century B.C. this identifying feature is for some reason abruptly dropped, the new jar is stamped, at the base of one handle, with the 5th century coin type of Chios, a sphinx with a wine jar, apparently so that it will not fail to be recognized while its shape is still unfamiliar. The amphora represented on coin (49) and stamp (48) is of the old shape with the swelling, known in the Persian empire, in Egypt and on the north shores of the Black Sea. The last of the 5th century series (45, right end) illustrates an item 'Chian amphoras' in the lists of property confiscated from Alcibiades and his fellows in 415 B.C. (see Picture Book No. 4, under 7). During the 4th century (46), the Chian loses its button toe, the shoulder sharpens, the neck continues to lengthen and the mouth begins to project higher above the handles, until we reach the sharp-pointed amphoras of the Hellenistic period, early and late (47). Matching these in sharp shoulder, color of clay and other details is the small one-handled Chian container (50), called *lagynos*, or *lagoena* as we know from the Roman poet Plautus who flourished when this jug was new, in the late 3rd century B.C.; see his *Curculio*, lines 78–79. The wine of Chios was perhaps the most famous of all Greek wines.

48, 49. Stamp and silver coin of Chios. Third quarter of the 5th century B.C. (2:1). In 43 a similar stamp may be seen on the new-style Chian (right).

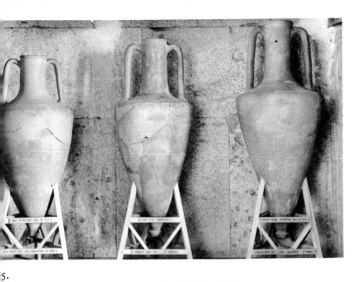

5.

44–47. Dated series of Chian amphoras from the Agora Excavations. Second half of 6th to early 1st century B.C. The last jar in 44 and the first in 45 (stamped) are from the same deposit as those in 43. Compare 46 with the coin on the front cover.

46. 4th century B.C.

47. 3rd and 1st centuries B.C.

50. Stamped Chian lagynos. *Ca.* 200 B.C. (under 1:5).

51. Silver coin of Chios. 1st century B.C. (2:1).

52. Lesbian (?) of the early and late 5th century B.C. and Thasian of the 4th and 3rd.

53. Lesbian (?) earmark (1:2).

Lesbos and Thasos were also known for their fine wines which improved with age; see 28–30, devices for state control in the Thasian wine industry. Of the amphoras attributed to Lesbos (52, left), the larger ones are of a dark gray clay, an effect of special firing and typical of much pottery from Lesbos. Apart from the general shape and color of these jars, they are identified as a group by an earmark (53)—a small tail of the clay of the handle which lies out below it on the shoulder of the jar.

Thasian amphoras (52, right) are plainly labelled *thasion*, in full or abbreviated, in their stamps (54, 55); the two here illustrated are of the kind, datable after about 340 B.C., in which only one name is mentioned, apparently that of a controller of production; compare 28, of the early 4th century, which has two names. The clay of Thasian jars is reddish, with a great deal of mica. In both the Lesbian and the Thasian groups in 52, the lefthand jar is fractional in size as well as earlier in date, which further accounts for the difference in shape.

The wine of Kos was admired, but it was a relatively inexpensive grade, bought in larger quantities; like Rhodian and Knidian, it sometimes had sea water added as a preservative. Koan stamps occasionally include the letters KO, short for *koïon* (58), but the jars have been chiefly

54, 55. Stamps of the Thasian jars in 52. The bow recalls the types of Herakles (27, 28).

56. Koan, 3rd to 1st centuries B.C. All have double handles like 58 and 59.

identified by the Koan coin symbols (59) and the many Koan names in the stamps on the very distinctive double-barrelled handles (58, 59). The dated series of jars in 56 and 57 (of which only the first two are stamped) show a tendency to grow tall and narrow. An offset at the base of the neck is an early feature. Later it is repeated at the base of the shoulder. The double handles make Koans easy to recognize, but their pale greenish surface color is also to be noticed, because there are some dark-colored amphoras that seem to be imitation Koan; see next page.

57. Koan, 1st century A.D.

58. Handle of Koan jar of Dorimachos.

59. Koan handle stamped with crab and club, symbols on coins of Kos.

60. Pseudo-Koan. 1st century A.D.

61. Wineshop in Pompeii.

62. Rhodian. Late 3rd and early 1st centuries B.C. and early 2nd century A.D. The first two are dated by their stamps in the terms of Thestor and of Archembrotos. The horned jar is unstamped.

Here in 60 are three samples from a filling of the 1st century A.D. at the Athenian Agora. All three have double-barrelled handles and offsets just below the handles. Thus they are like contemporary Koan (57), though much less elegant. They are dark in color; the middle one is distinctly red. A number of similar amphoras found at Pompeii (e.g. 61), where they had been covered by the eruption of Vesuvius in 79 A.D., confirm the date; these were perhaps containers for the Italian imitation of Koan wine, for which a recipe has come down to us from the Romans (Cato, *De Agricultura*, 112).

The horned handles on the 1st century Koan (57) and on some of the pseudo-Koan echo the contemporary Rhodian; see the right end of 62. Here the lifting and sharpening of the angles of the handles and bowing out of the shafts have been gradually developed; see the two preceding in 62 and then 22 (twenty years still earlier) where the curve is softer. Still earlier Rhodian handles have no angle but a rounded arch. The peglike toe and simple rim of the

63. Ancient cellar in Rhodes. The top of one handle cleared below, left, bore a rose stamp of Xenotimos, 3rd century B.C.

familiar Rhodian amphora are known as early as about 275 B.C. Some quite distinct shapes (not illustrated here), which at first ran parallel with this in Rhodes, later went out of use, and stamps on the tops of the handles of the chosen form were quite often embellished, by about 250 B.C., with the coin symbol, the Rhodian 'rose'. For coin symbols in Rhodian stamps, see 23–25.

At home in Rhodes, local containers, if not local produce, seem to have been the rule, since less than five per cent of the stamped handles found in the island are from foreign jars. There have been some remarkable discoveries here of amphoras in their ancient places of storage. The most extraordinary is a rockcut cellar, within the city of Rhodes, cleared in the summer of 1960 by the Greek Archaeological Service (63). When all the earth covering was removed, there proved to be 137 Rhodian jars in rows, resting on their mouths. Were these empties? Or had they been laid down with wine in them, inverted so that the moisture would keep the corks swollen tight? More exciting to the archaeologist are certain questions which can be resolved as soon as the jars can be taken up and studied, in particular, what combinations of dating and endorsing names do their pairs of stamps (cf. 23, 25) provide? On such combinations depends the detailed dating of Rhodian amphoras.

64. Knidian. 3rd to 1st century B.C. (all stamped) and early 2nd A.D.

Potter and dating official are usually named in the same stamp on Knidian jars (21, 39, 65, and the drawing on the title page). Whole jars retaining both handles date for us in ancient terms the annually appointed pairs of commissioners who evidently helped to administer Knidos as part of a Roman province in the late 2nd and early 1st centuries B.C. For instance 39 and 40, of which duplicates appear one on either handle of a whole jar, name (39) a potter Aineas with his fishhook device, the term of Sosiphron (*epi Sosiphronos*), and the jar itself, a *knidion*, also (40) the commissioners Kydosthenes and Demetrios. Wherever tests can be made, jars dated in this term name the same pair. Certain earlier stamps reflect an administrative change of historically known date, the Rhodian occupation of Knidos in 188–167 B.C., and so help our chronology. In Knidian stamps, though the word *knidion* usually appears, coin symbols of Knidos are often used, especially the facing head of a bull (65).

Again in 64 one sees the tendency of jars to grow narrower. The stamped tops of the handles, at first long and sloping, shorten and become arched. The clay is red, overlaid in the second jar with a cream slip, no doubt in imitation of Rhodian amphoras, since this jar is of the occupation period.

The distinctive Knidian ring around the toe marks a series of small jars of the 4th and 5th centuries A.D. of which one is shown to the right in 66. Are they the *knidia* mentioned in contemporary papyri?

65. Knidian stamp.
About 90 B.C.

66. Small *knidia* (?).
1st century B.C. (left)
and 4th century A.D.
About 1:12.

Many kinds of containers are mentioned in papyri, the business records and correspondence of Greek merchants and estate-owners in Egypt, preserved to this day in the dry climate. The jars are often referred to by their local names, 'Knidian', 'Chian' and the like. Certain other names have puzzled scholars attempting to estimate the price of wine implied by these records. Among these, *spatheion*, 'blade', a curious description of a container, could surely not find a more likely identification than in the long slim jars in 67. These jars are interesting for another reason: hundreds like them were used in the construction of the roofs of three Early Christian buildings in Ravenna, Italy, taking the place of bricks or concrete, no doubt for lightness. See 68; on the other two buildings, domes were made by laying similar jars, toe in mouth, in circles or spirals of diminishing size.

67. *Spatheia* (?) and a small jar of common type perhaps from Egypt. 5th to 6th century A.D.

68. *Spatheia* (?) used in roof construction. Tomb of Galla Placidia, Ravenna. 5th century A.D.

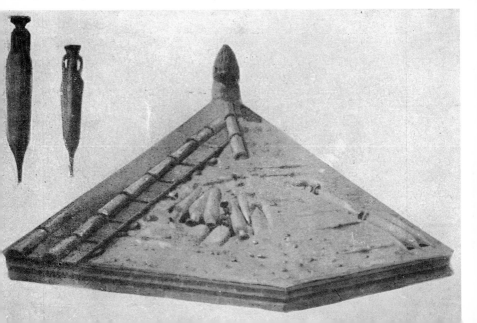

Our chronology has been built up primarily from contexts of discovery of hundreds of jars and of thousands of stamped fragments, some from cities whose date of destruction is known, a great many from carefully excavated and recorded ancient fillings. Patterns of shape development, learned from setting well-dated jars in a row, help to check the results. The interconnection of names of makers and dating authorities cited in the stamps fills out and consolidates the sequences.

The picture puzzle is still being fitted together, but already there are rather few stamped handles to which a rough date at least cannot be attributed. These very common finds now often serve to date excavated ancient levels and associated objects or buildings more narrowly than can be done by any other available means.

To the economic historian we are now in a position to offer information about the wine trade based on impressive figures and reliable dates. For example, our evidence indicates that Knidos in the late 2nd and early 1st centuries B.C. was the chief source of cheap wine imported by Athens and by the great commercial port of Delos then controlled by Athens; whereas imports of Knidian wine by Alexandria had fallen off sharply in the late 2nd century. The statement is based on readings of some 34,000 Knidian stamped handles in Athens, Delos and Alexandria, and on a particularly well-established chronology, drawn largely from many good contexts at the Agora excavations.

These dry studies will be increasingly supplemented by the divers. As they range further and with better techniques along the shores of the ancient world, through their reports lost cargoes will mark for us the paths of ancient trade.

69. Roman merchantman with a deck load of amphoras. Mosaic in North Africa.

NOTES ON ILLUSTRATIONS

Inventory numbers preceded by P or SS designate material found in the excavations of the Athenian Agora and now housed in the Stoa of Attalos. Stamps and coins are shown at about actual size unless otherwise indicated in the legends. Beginning with 22, amphoras without human scale are at about 1:15, save in 61, 63, 66 and 68. Most are from an exhibition in one of the ancient rooms of the Stoa. Since the inventory numbers of these jars appear below them in the photographs, they are not repeated in the following notes.

For the use of supplementary material, grateful acknowledgement is made to the museums whose names are given below. Particular thanks are due to the Greek Archaeological Service and to Dr. John Kondis for permission to publish 63.

Cover. Coin in private possession.

Inside cover. Photograph by John Cochran, kindness of Stanton Waterman. From the investigations by Peter Throckmorton of ancient wrecks near Budrum (Halikarnassos), Turkey, 1959; see *National Geographic Magazine*, May, 1960, p. 693.

Design on title page. Drawing by Piet de Jong of Knidian Type 125, from two examples at the Agora.

1. In the foreground, SS 9743, Knidian. 2nd century B.C. For stamp, see 21.
2. Peiraeus, Museum of Antiquities. Part of Attic (?) jar. 5th century B.C.
3. Sarasota, Florida, Ringling Museum. Rhodian jar. 2nd century B.C.
4. M. G. Lefebvre, *Le Tombeau de Petosiris*, Cairo, 1924, pl. XII.
5. Oinochoe, P 10408. C. G. Boulter, *Hesperia*, XXXII, 1963, pp. 131–132 and pl. 49, no. 13.
6. Jar, P 1253. *Hesperia*, VII, 1938, p. 379, fig. 14. Stand, P 15914.
7. J. D. Beazley, *Greek Vases in Poland*, Oxford, 1928, pl. 24.
8. *Zeitschrift für Ägyptische Sprache*, XXXIV–XXXVI, 1896, 1898, pl. XVII.
9. Oxford, Ashmolean Museum, 1884,583.
10. Ficoroni Cista. E. Pfuhl, *Malerei und Zeichnung der Griechen*, Munich, 1923, pp. 253–254.
11. Sir Flinders Petrie, *Beth Pelet I*, London, 1930, pl. VIII, Tomb 550.
12. P. E. Newberry, *The Life of Rekhmara*, London, 1900, pl. XIII.
13. *Hesperia*, IX, 1940, p. 283, fig. 24. To the right, P 15358.
14. C. F. A. Schaeffer, *Ugaritica*, II, Paris, 1949, pl. XXXI.
15. Mycenae 54–601. *Annual of the British School at Athens*, L, 1955, pl. 20, b.
16. N. de G. Davies, *The Tomb of Nakht at Thebes*, New York, 1917, pl. XXVI.
17. J. D. S. Pendlebury, *The City of Akhenaten*, III, Oxford, 1951, p. 182, fig. 23.
18. From the excavations of Lachish. Courtesy of the Wellcome-Marston Expedition; kindness of Miss Olga Tufnell.
19. Sir Arthur Evans, *The Palace of Minos*, IV, London, 1935, p. 731, fig. 714.
20. British Museum, *Catalogue of the Greek Coins, Macedonia*, etc., London, 1879, p. 135, I. For a photograph of this coin, see back cover.
21. One of two duplicate impressions on the two handles of SS 9743.
22. From Agora deposit B 13:7. SS 7582, to the right, is endorsed by Menekrates and dated by Mytion.
23. SS 7583, stamps on incomplete jar from Agora deposit B 13:7.
24. British Museum, *Catalogue of the Greek Coins, Caria*, etc., London, 1897, pl. XXXVIII, 8.
25. SS 7584, stamps on much-restored jar from Agora deposit B 13:7.
26. Rhodes, Archaeological Museum, Rhodian jar from the Villanova deposit.
27. A. B. West, *Fifth and Fourth Century Gold Coins from the Thracian Coast*, New York, 1929, pl. III, 13A. New photograph from a cast, kindness of the American Numismatic Society and Margaret Thompson.
28. Corinth C 31–468. C. Roebuck, *Corinth*, XIV, 1951, p. 137, fig. 26, 87.

29. *Bulletin de Correspondence Hellénique*, LXXIX, 1955, p. 365, fig. 37.
30. J. Pouilloux, *Recherches sur l'Histoire et les Cultes de Thasos*, I, Paris, 1954, pl. v, 3. Photograph kindness of M. Pouilloux.
31. Corinth C 47–838b, C 47–840, from well in Southeast Building.
32. A. Maiuri, *Pompeii*, 2nd ed., Novara, 1943, p. 109.
34. From a map prepared by Phyllis Gomme.
35. From Agora deposits G 11:3 (jar to left) and Q 12:3. Others from the latter deposit are the second Chian and the first Lesbian in 44, 52.
36. SS 8602, SS 7918, P 19120, SS 7319. The middle two are from Agora deposit N 20:4.
38. From Agora deposit C 9:7.
39. Athens, National Museum, KT 95 EM 3.
40. Athens, National Museum, KT 1555 EM 2.
41. SS 6598, stamp on shoulder.
42. From Agora deposit D 15:3. Corcyrean or Corinthian and Attic (?).
43. From Agora deposit R 13:4.
44. A–P 2422, first jar to left, from excavations by O. Broneer on the North Slope of the Akropolis. *Hesperia*, IX, 1940, p. 258, fig. 61, 336.
46. P 25947. From Agora deposit F 17:3, construction filling.
47. P 1114, P 19120 (also in 36).
48. Stamp at base of handle of SS 1838.
49. Cambridge, Fitzwilliam Museum. S. W. Grose, *Catalogue of the McClean Collection of Greek Coins*, III, Cambridge, 1929, no. 8361. New photograph by kindness of Graham Pollard, Assistant Keeper.
50. SS 10259. *Hesperia*, Suppl. X, 1956, pl. 73.
51. Coin in private possession.
53. Detail of P 12789.
54, 55. Stamps, P 675 and SS 8932, respectively; cf. A.-M. and A. Bon, *Les timbres amphoriques de Thasos*, Paris, 1957, nos. 718d and 146.
58, 59. Respectively SS 12618, SS 12048. 3rd or early 2nd century B.C.
60. From Agora deposit N 20:2.
61. *Notizie degli Scavi*, IX, 1912, p. 114, fig. 11.
62. Jar 1 (SS 9991), *Hesperia*, XXXII, 1963, p. 323, fig. 1, no. 9. Jar 2, *Transactions of the American Philosophical Society*, LV, 1965, p. 9, fig. 3, A.
63. Excavations beside the Hotel Soleil, in the city of Rhodes, May, 1960.
64. For a descriptive list of items in this picture, with commentary, see *Exploration archéologique de Délos*, XXVII, Paris, 1970, pp. 317–318 with note 2.
65. Athens, National Museum, KT 486 EM I.
66. P 10790, left, and P 25183.
68. *Bollettino d'Arte*, VIII, 1914, p. 9, fig. 38.
69. Mosaic at Tebessa, North Africa. 3rd (?) century A.D. Kindness of P. Cintas and L. Casson; cf. also *Archaeology*, X, 1957, p. 251.
Back cover. British Museum, Macedonian coin in 20. Ca. 500 B.C. Cf. Svoronos in *Journal International d'Archéologie Numismatique*, 1919, pp. 63ff. Date, reference and new photograph, kindness of G. K. Jenkins.

Addendum 1979. For the basis of some revisions in this booklet, see 1) V. R. Grace in *Athenische Mitteilungen* 89, 1974, pp. 193–200 (changes in 3rd century B.C. chronology); and 2) Y. Garlan in the forthcoming *Bulletin de correspondence hellénique*, Suppl.V (new light on the function of persons named in Thasian one-name stamps, cf. 54, 55). I am grateful to M. Garlan for information in advance of publication.